LIFE

OF

St. Margaret

QUEEN OF SCOTLAND

BY

TURGOT, BISHOP OF ST. ANDREWS

Translated from the Latin by

WILLIAM FORBES-LEITH, S.J.

SECOND EDITION.

THE FRATERY OF DUNFERMLINE ABBEY

EDINBURGH: WILLIAM PATERSON

MDCCCLXXXIV

St Margaret's Oratory in Edinburgh Castle.

Restored in 1853 by command of Her Majesty Queen Victoria.

CONTENTS.

6   Contents.

CHAPTER III.

CHAPTER IV.

ILLUSTRATIONS.

I. St Margaret's Oratory in Edinburgh Castle.

Frontispiece

The complete restoration of the oratory was effected in 1853, by command of Her Majesty Queen Victoria. The modern western entrance was built up, and an ancien. one re-opened at the north-west corner of the nave. Here a new doorway was placed in the same style with the rest of the building. The three small round-headed windows were filled in with stained glass—the light in the south side of the apse representing St Margaret; the two in the side of the nave showing her husband, King Malcolm Canmore, and their son St David; and the light in the west gable of the nave having a cross and the sacred monogram with this inscription :—*Hæc ædicula olim Beatæ Margaretæ Reginæ Scotiæ, quæ obiit M.XCIII., ingratæ patriæ negligentiâ lapsa, Victoriæ Reginæ prognatæ auspiciis restituta, A.D. M.DCCCLIII.*

II. St Margaret's Tomb, Dunfermline Abbey . 22

In 1250 the remains of St Margaret were transferred from the old original tomb, in the now western church, to the splendid new tomb specially erected to receive them in the "Lady Aisle" of the then recently-built choir. From 1250 to 1560, *lights* were kept perpetually burning before this tomb, as also on each side of the shrine, of which frequent mention is made in the *Register of Dunfermline*. This tomb appears to have been destroyed by the reformers on the 28th of March, 1560, or by the falling of the walls shortly after that period. All that now remains is the double plinth of limestone, in a dilapidated condition, now outside the area of the present

8   Illustrations.

church (on the east). On the upper plinth are still to be seen six circular indentures, from which rose "*six slender shafts of shapely stone,*" that supported a highly-ornamented canopy. In the centre of the second or upper plinth stood St Margaret's shrine. (*E. Henderson, "Annals of Dunfermline,*" p. 86.)

The Royal Palace appears to have been much enlarged and thoroughly repaired about 1540. Large mullioned windows were introduced into the original architecture. The present upper storey with bay windows was then added to the building. The west wall overlooking the glen is 205 feet in length.

VIGNETTES.

This is situated but a short distance up the glen from the royal abode. According to tradition, St Margaret often resorted thither for private devotion. The custom of retiring for a time to a cave was very common among the British and Scottish Saints. (*Cf.* "*Historians of Scotland,*" vol. v., 345.)

INTRODUCTION.

THE great loss sustained by the English in the death of Harold was their deprivation of a national leader. Harold's brothers had fallen with him in the field at Senlac. Of his sons no mention was ever made. Once more men looked to the royal line, and the Ætheling Edgar, grandson of Edmund Ironside, whilst still a boy, was chosen king. Such a leader only weakened the national cause; and no sooner did William approach the city of London than all opposition faded away. The northern Earls, Edwin and Morkar, would hazard nothing, and, dismayed by William's advance, made haste to retreat northwards. The bishops, after a brief display of resistance, counselled submission to him, and at Christmas his coronation finally made him King of England.

Thus ended the Saxon's main struggle for freedom. But the country was by no means conquered. East of a line from Norwich to Dorset, William was king. All north and west of that was yet to be won. The English, however, felt that they were almost conquered, and the schemes they formed for their deliverance were wild and desperate. The signal for a general revolt came from Swegen, King of Denmark, on the appearance of his fleet at the mouth of the Humber in 1068. All northern, western, and south-western England rose as one man. The outbreak was heralded by the storming of York, and by the slaughter of three thousand Normans who formed its garrison. The news of this massacre reached William as he was hunting in the forest of Dean, and, giving way to a wild outburst of wrath, he swore to avenge himself on the North. But wrath went hand-in-hand with the coolest statesmanship. The real enemies to be disposed of were the Danes. These William bought off, and then turning upon the disorganised rebels, he defeated them in detail by a series of skilful marches. The English submitted, and left the Normans undisputed masters of the kingdom. Edgar the Ætheling, with his mother Agatha, his sisters Margaret and Christina, and the last relics of the English nobility,[1] resolved to sail for Wearmouth, and to seek a shelter at the court of Malcolm, King of Scotland. They could hardly have expected to find the man who

[1] These were the English Thanes: Archill, the great Northumbrian Thane, to whom Malcolm granted large territories in Dumbarton, compensating the spoliation he had sustained from the Conqueror: Merlesweyn, Siward-Barn, Alfwin, all of whom can be recognised as landed men under Malcolm, and whose descendants subsequently appear high on the roll of Scotland's territorial aristocracy. Tradition also mentions the families of Lyndesay, Vaux, Ramsay, Lovel, Towers, Preston, Sandiland, Wisheart, Soulis, Maxwell, Crichton, Giffard, Maule, Leslie and Borthwick, established in the Scottish dominions during Malcolm's reign. (Sir Francis Palgrave, " History of England and Normandy," vol. iv., p. 335. Cf. Hailes, " Ann. Scot.," vol. i. pp. 7, 8 : the " Scots Compendium," etc.)

was to have been their host, in the very act of ravaging their native country; but this savage occupation in no way lessened his friendly feelings towards them. He met them in person, he gave them the most hearty reception, and bade them dwell in his realm as long as it might please them.[1] They sailed towards Scotland; while he went on with the harrying of Northumberland. For when he was still at Wearmouth, news reached him that Gospatric, William's earl in Northumberland, had burst into Malcolm's Cumbrian province, had devastated the land with fire and sword, and had returned with great spoil to the old fortress of the Northumbrian kings at Bambrough, which he held as his headquarters. When the tidings of Gospatric's inroad into

[1] Edgar and his suite were not unknown to the Scottish king. Deprived of his father's protection in early youth, "Malcolm grew up into manhood under the Confessor's benign protection, his benefactor and his suzerain, standing before the Confessor's throne, consorting with the Confessor's knights, sitting at the Confessor's table." (Sir Francis Palgrave, "History of England and Normandy," vol. iv., p. 311.)

Cumberland were brought to Malcolm, he was filled with wrath, and issued orders such as William never gave. From that day forward none of English race were to be spared; the remnant that the Norman had left were to pay for the exploit of their Earl by death or hopeless slavery. The word was given, and it was carried out to the letter by the ruthless marauders to whom it was addressed. The old men and women were slaughtered, as Simeon of Durham puts it, like swine for the banquet.[1] Young men and maidens, and all of age and strength to be useful in slavery, were driven in fetters to the land of bondage.[2] Many sank through fatigue, some of them never to rise again; those in whom life was left found no pity, but were hurried on all the more unsparingly at the merciless bidding of Malcolm. Thus, we are told, was Scotland filled with English slaves of either sex. There was not a village, there was not even a

[1] "Simeonis Dunelmensis Opera," p. 88, Surtees Society.
[2] *Ibid.*

house so poor but could boast of some English captive held in thraldom.[1]

While Malcolm was still making his fearful march homewards, rich with the human spoil of noble England, the English exiles had reached Scotland in safety by sea. Some of the party soon returned to share the dangers of the insurgents at Ely.[2] But the Ætheling and his family paid Malcolm a longer visit, and Margaret, the sister of Edgar, was now entreated by the King to accept his hand. Both the sisters of Edgar, however, were inclined to a religious life.[3] Margaret, her brother, and all her companions, at the first utterly refused to hearken to the King's suit. But the love of Malcolm was not to be withstood. "He dealt with her brother till he said Yea; for in truth he durst not say otherwise, seeing they had come into Malcolm's power."[4]

[1] "Simeonis Dunelmensis Opera," p. 88, Surtees Society.
[2] Freeman, "History of the Norman Conquest," vol. iv. p. 468.
[3] Christina became Abbess of an English monastery.
[4] "Chron. Wig.," 1067. The marriage took place about 1070. Cf. E. Freeman, vol. iv., appendix B.B., p. 782.

"It was," says Mr Freeman, "a good day for Malcolm and for Scotland when Margaret was persuaded or constrained to exchange the easy self-dedication of the cloister for the harder task of doing her duty in that state of life to which it had pleased God to call her.[1] Margaret became the mirror of wives, mothers, and queens, and none ever more worthily earned the honours of Saintship. Her gentle influence reformed whatever needed to be reformed in her husband, and none laboured more diligently for the advance of temporal and spiritual enlightenment in her adopted country. . . . There was indeed no need for Margaret to bring a new religion into Scotland, but she gave a new life to the religion which she found existing there. She became the correspondent of Lanfranc, and her life was written by the

[1] No royal marriage was ever more important in its results for England. "It was through Margaret that the old kingly blood of England passed into the veins of the descendants of the Conqueror. The tree returns to the root when Henry the First marries Matilda the daughter of Margaret; it bears leaves at the birth of her children." (E. Freeman, "History of the Norman Conquest," vol. iii. p. 12.)

holy Prior and Bishop Turgot.[1]   It is one of the
most interesting pieces that we have as a personal and ecclesiastical biography."[2]   As one of
our most distinguished Scotch writers truly
observes :—" There is perhaps no more beautiful
character recorded in history than that of Margaret.   For purity of motives, for an earnest
desire to benefit the people among whom her lot
was cast, for a deep sense of religion and great
personal piety, for the unselfish performance of
whatever duty lay before her, and for entire self-
abnegation, she is unsurpassed, and the chroniclers of the time[3] all bear testimony to her exalted
character."[4]

Turgot's Memoir of St Margaret is the only
authentic account we have of her life.   " My

[1] Turgot, Prior of Durham, was consecrated Bishop of St
Andrews at York on the 1st August 1109 ; he died on 31st
of August 1115.
[2] E. Freeman, " History of the Norman Conquest," vol.
iv. p. 510.
[3] " Orderic Vital," b. viii. c. 20; " Anglo-Saxon Chronicle,"
Thorpe's edition, vol. ii. p. 172.
[4] W. F. Skene, " Celtic Scotland," vol. ii. p. 344.

evidence," says Turgot, "is especially trustworthy, since (thanks to her great and familiar intercourse with me) I am acquainted with the most part of her secrets." As the late Dr Forbes truly remarks, "there is an atmosphere of calm unexcited truthfulness about the narrative, as well as an absence of the mythical, which commends it to us as the work of an eminently truth-loving man, and the incidental allusions to the current history bear the test of all that we know of the times."[1]

It is also "full of instructive notices of the state of the Scottish Church and kingdom at the epoch of the Norman conquest of England, and *it supplies us with the first really authentic history of Scotland* after the notices in Adamnan and Bæda, The Pictish Chronicle, and the Book of Deer."[2]

For the following translation of the life gene-

---

[1] Dr A. Penrose Forbes, "Calendars of the Scottish Saints," p. 390.
[2] *Ibid.*, p. 386.

rally ascribed to Turgot we have used the Latin text printed in the *Acta Sanctorum*, vol. ii., 328 (10th June). Papebroch, who edited it, contends that it was written by Theodoric. His arguments, however, do not seem to us very conclusive. According to Lord Hailes and other writers, it is probable that Theodoric is either another name for Turgot, or that the name of Theodoric, instead of Turgot, has been prefixed to the Saint's life by some copier.[1]

[1] Of the " Life of Queen Margaret " but one copy exists in manuscript in this kingdom, in a folio volume on vellum, of the latter part of the twelfth century, Cotton. Tiberius, D. III., which was much injured by the great fire in the British Museum. The same life is printed in the *Acta Sanctorum*, in Pinkerton's Lives of Scottish Saints, in the publications of the Surtees Society (1868). An abridgment exists in the MS. Cotton. Tiberius, E. 1, a folio in double columns, also injured by fire, and dates from the beginning of the fourteenth century.

On the question of the authorship of this work, see the preface to " Simeonis Dunelmensis Opera," Surtees Society, 1868.

THE PROLOGUE.

O the honourable and excellent Matilda, queen of the English, T[urgot],[1] servant of the servants of St Cuthbert, sends the blessing of peace and health in this present life, and in that which is to come the chief good of all good things.

§ 1. You have, by the request you made, commanded me (since a request of yours is to me a command) that I should narrate for you the particulars of the life of your mother, whose memory is held in veneration. How acceptable that life was to God you have often heard by the concordant praise of many. You remind me how in this matter my evidence is especially trustworthy, since (thanks to her great and familiar intercourse with me) you have understood that I

---

[1] *Theodoricus* in the "Acta Sanctorum," and in Pinkerton's edition. In the Cotton. MS., the words *Per Turgotum Dunelmensem* are added at the end of the paragraph, in a hand of the seventeenth century.

am acquainted with the most part of her secrets. These your commands and wishes I willingly obey; nay, more, I venerate them exceedingly, and I respectfully congratulate you—whom the King of the Angels has raised to the rank of Queen of England—that you desire not only to hear about the life of your mother, who ever yearned after the Kingdom of the Angels, but further, to have it continually before your eyes in writing, that so, although you were but little familiar with her face, you might at least have a perfect acquaintance with her virtues.

For my part, my own wish inclines me to do what you bid, but I have, I confess, a lack of ability: as the materials, in truth, for this undertaking are more than my writing or my words can avail to set forth.

§ 2. So I am in two minds, and drawn two ways at once. On the one hand, the greatness of the subject makes me shrink from obeying; on the other, I dare not refuse because of the authority of you who command me, and the memory of her of whom I am to speak. I cannot do justice to my subject, yet my duty is to make it known so far as I can. I owe this to the love I have for her, and to the obedience which is due from me to you. I trust that the grace of the Holy Spirit, which gave her such powers for good, will to me vouchsafe also the ability to recount them. "The Lord shall give the word to them that preach good tidings with great power." (Ps. lxvii. 12.)[1]

§ 3. In the first place, then, it is my wish that you should know, and others through you, that were I to attempt to recount all I could tell to her honour, I might be suspected, while praising your mother, to be really flattering your own queenly dignity. But far be it from my grey hairs to mingle falsehood with the virtues of such a woman as she was, in unfolding which I profess—as God is my Witness and my Judge—that I add nothing to the truth. On the contrary, I suppress many things, fearing that they might appear incredible, and I might be charged (as the orator says) with decking out the crow in the plumage of the swan.

---

[1] "Open thy mouth wide, and I will fill it" (Ps. lxxxvii. 10). "For no one can fail in the Word who believes in the Word." "In the beginning was the Word, and the Word was God" (St John i. 1).

ST MARGARET'S TOMB, DUNFERMLINE ABBEY.

CHAPTER I.

§ 4.

MANY, as we read, have got their name from a quality of their mind, so that in their regard there is shown a correspondence between the word forming their name and the grace they have received. Peter was so named from "the Rock," that is Christ, in token of the firmness of his faith; John, which means "the grace of God," from his contemplation of the Divinity, and his prerogative of Divine love; and the sons of Zebedee were styled Boanerges, that is, "the sons of thunder," because they thundered forth the preaching of the Gospel. The same thing was true of this virtuous woman, for the fairness which was pre-shadowed in her name was eclipsed by the surpassing beauty of her soul. She was called Margaret, and in the sight of God she showed herself to be a pearl, precious in faith and works. She was indeed a pearl to you, to me, to all of us, yea, to Christ Himself, and being Christ's she is all the more ours now that she has left us, having been taken to the Lord. This pearl, I repeat, has been removed from the dunghill of the present world, and now she shines in her place among the jewels of the Eternal King. Of this no one, I think, will doubt, who reads the following narrative of her life and death. When I call to mind her conversations with us, seasoned as they were with the salt of wisdom; when I bethink me of her tears wrung from the compunction of her heart; when I regard her staidness and the even balance of her manners; when I remember her affability and prudence, I rejoice while I lament, and in lamenting I rejoice. I rejoice, because she has passed away to God, after whom she yearned; and I grieve because I am not rejoicing along with her, in the heavenly places. I rejoice for her, because she now sees, in the land of the living, those good things of the Lord in which she had believed; but for myself I mourn, because so long as I suffer the miseries of this mortal life in the land of the dead, · so long am I constrained to exclaim day by day : " Unhappy man that I am, who shall deliver me from the body of this death !"[1]

§ 5. Since, then, I am about to speak of that nobility of the mind which she had in Christ, it is fitting that something should be premised as to her nobility according to this world. Her grandfather was that King Edmund who had earned an honourable surname from his matchless valour, for he was staunch in fight and not to be overcome by his enemies ; and therefore he was called in English " The Ironside." His brother on his father's side, but not on his mother's, was the most religious and meek Edward, who proved himself a father to his country, which, like another Solomon (that is, a lover of peace), he protected rather by peace than arms. His was a spirit which overcame anger, despised avarice, and was utterly free from pride. And no wonder ; for as from his ancestors he drew the glory of his

[1] Rom. vii. 24.

kingly rank, so from them too he inherited his nobility of life. He was descended from Edgar, King of the English, and Richard, Count of the Normans, his grandfathers on either side; not only most illustrious, but also most religious men. Of Edgar it may briefly be said (if we would do justice to his worth as well in this world as in Christ), that he was marked out beforehand as a king at once just and peaceful. For at his birth St Dunstan heard the holy angels rejoicing in heaven and singing with great joy: "Let there be peace, let there be joy in the Church of the English as long as this new-born child shall hold his kingdom and Dunstan run the course of this mortal life."

§ 6. Richard also, father to Emma the mother of this Edward, was an ancestor worthy of so illustrious a grandchild; he was a man of energy and worthy of all praise. None of his forefathers had attained greater prosperity and honour in his earldom of Normandy, nor was any of them more fervent in religion. Though of great wealth, he was poor in spirit, like a second David; though raised to be lord over his people, he was the most humble servant of the servants of Christ. Among other memorials of his love of religion, this devout worshipper founded the noble monastery of Fécamp, in which it was his frequent custom to stay with the religious. There, in habit a secular but in heart a monk, he placed the food of the brethren on the table where they were eating their silent meals and served them with drink ; so that, according to the Scriptures, " The greater he was, by so much the more did he humble himself to all."[1] If anyone wishes to be more fully acquainted with his works of magnificence and virtue, let him read the book called " The Acts of the Normans,"[2] which contains his history. Edward, the grandchild of such forefathers, did in no way degenerate from their renown and excellence. As already has been said, he was the brother of King Edmund on the father's side only ; from whose son came Margaret, who by the splendour of her merits completes the glory of this illustrious pedigree.

§ 7. Whilst Margaret was yet in the flower of youth, she began to lead a very strict life, to

[1] Eccl. iii. 20.
[2] See Duchesne, " Historiæ Normannorum Scriptores."

love God above all things, to employ herself in the study of the Divine writings, and therein with joy to exercise her mind. Her understanding was keen to comprehend any matter, whatever it might be; to this was joined a great tenacity of memory, enabling her to store it up, along with a graceful flow of language to express it.

§ 8. While thus she was meditating upon the law of the Lord day and night, and, like another Mary sitting at His feet, delighted to hear His word, rather in obedience to the will of her friends than to her own, yea by the appointment of God, she was married to Malcolm, son of King Duncan, the most powerful king of the Scots. But although she was compelled to do as the world does, she thought it beneath her dignity to fix her affection upon the things of the world, and thus good works delighted her more than riches. By means of her temporal possession she earned for herself the rewards of heaven; for there, where her heart was, she had placed her treasure also. And since before all things she sought the kingdom of God and His justice,[1] the bountiful grace of the Almighty freely

1 St. Matth. vi. 33.

added to her honours and riches in abundance. This prudent queen directed all such things as it was fitting for her to regulate; the laws of the realm were administered by her counsel; by her care the influence of religion was extended, and the people rejoiced in the prosperity of their affairs. Nothing was firmer than her fidelity, steadier than her favour, or juster than her decisions; nothing was more enduring than her patience, graver than her advice, or more pleasant than her conversation.

§ 9. She had no sooner attained this eminent dignity, than she built an eternal memorial of her name and devotion in the place where her nuptials had been held.[1] The noble church which she erected there in honour of the Holy Trinity was to serve a threefold purpose; it was intended for the redemption of the king's soul, for the good of her own, and for securing to her children prosperity in the present life and in that which is to come. This church she beautified with rich gifts of various kinds, amongst which, as is well known, were many vessels of pure and

[1] Dunfermline.

solid gold for the sacred service of the altar, about
which I can speak with the greater certainty since,
by the queen's orders, I myself, for a long time,
had all of them under my charge. She also placed
there a cross of priceless value, bearing the figure
of our Saviour, which she had caused to be
covered with the purest gold and silver studded
with gems, a token even to the present day of the
earnestness of her faith. She left proofs of her
devotion and fervour in various other churches,
as witness the Church of St Andrews, in which
is preserved a most beautiful crucifix erected by
her there, and remaining even at the present day.
Her chamber was never without such objects,
those I mean which appertained to the dignity of
the divine service. It was, so to speak, a work-
shop of sacred art : in which copes for the cantors,
chasubles, stoles, altar-cloths, together with other
priestly vestments and church ornaments of an
admirable beauty, were always to be seen, either
already made, or in course of preparation.[1]

[1] Not only in Saxon or Celtic times, but until the Refor-
mation, one of the principal occupations of ladies was the em-

§ 10. These works were entrusted to certain women of noble birth and approved gravity of manners, who were thought worthy of a part in the queen's service. No men were admitted among them, with the exception only of such as she permitted to enter along with herself when she paid the women an occasional visit. No giddy pertness was allowed in them, no light familiarity between them and men; for the queen united so much strictness with her sweetness of temper, so great pleasantness even with her severity, that all who waited upon her,

broidering of exquisite vestments for churches, so that the poet of old thus addresses them :—

> " And ye, lovely ladies,
>   With your longe fyngres,
>   That ye have silk and sandel
>   To sowe when tyme is
>   Chesibles for chapelynes,
>   Churches to honoure."
>   (*Vision of Piers Plowman*, vol. i.
>   p. 117, ed. Wright.)

English ladies were so famous for embroidery in solid gold wire or gold thread, that it was called *Opus Anglicum*. (See Rock's Introduction to " Catalogue of Textile Fabrics in South Kensington Museum," and " Church of our Fathers," vol. ii. p. 276.)

men as well as women, loved her while they feared her, and in fearing loved her. Thus it came to pass that when she was present no one ventured to utter even one unseemly word, much less to do aught that was objectionable. There was a gravity in her very joy, and something stately in her anger. With her, mirth never expressed itself in fits of laughter, nor did displeasure kindle into fury. Sometimes she chid the faults of others—her own always—using that commendable severity tempered with justice which the Psalmist directs us unceasingly to employ, when he says, "Be ye angry, and sin not." Every action of her life was regulated by the balance of the nicest discretion, which impressed its own distinctive character upon each single virtue. When she spoke, her conversation was seasoned with the salt of wisdom; when she was silent, her silence was filled with good thoughts. So thoroughly did her outward bearing correspond with the staidness of her character that it seemed as if she had been from her very birth the pattern of a virtuous life. In fact, I may say, every word which she uttered, every act which she performed, shewed that she was meditating upon the things of heaven.

§ 11. Nor was she less careful about her children than she was about herself. She took all heed that they should be well brought up, and especially that they should be trained in virtue. Knowing that it is written : " He that spareth the rod hateth his son,"[1] she charged the governor who had the care of the nursery to curb the children, to scold them, and to whip them whenever they were naughty, as frolicsome childhood will often be. Thanks to their mother's religious care, her children surpassed in good behaviour many who were their elders ; they were always affectionate and peaceable among themselves, and everywhere the younger paid due respect to the elder. Thus it was that during the solemnities of the Mass, when they went up to make their offerings after their parents, never on any occasion did the younger venture to precede the elder ; the custom being for the elder to go before those younger according to the

---

[1] Prov. xiii. 24.

order of their birth.[1] She frequently called them
to her, and carefully instructed them about Christ
and the things of Christ, as far as their age
would permit, and she admonished them to love
Him always. "O, my children," said she, "fear
the Lord; for they who fear Him shall lack
nothing,[2] and if you love Him, He will give you,
my dear ones, prosperity in this life, and everlasting happiness with all the saints." Such were
this mother's wishes for her children, such her
admonitions, such her prayers for them, poured
out night and day with tears. She prayed that
they might confess their Maker through the faith
which works by love,[3] that confessing they
might worship Him, worshipping might love Him
in all things and above all things, and loving

---

[1] Royal and noble personages were accustomed to make
their offering at Mass. To do this they left their place, and
advancing to the altar or to the entrance of the chancel, laid
their gift in the hand of the celebrant or of the deacon. On
this subject see "History of the Holy Eucharist in Great
Britain," by Father Bridgett, vol. ii. p. 212 ; "Lay Folk's
Mass Book," edited by Canon Simmons, pp. 231-248.

[2] Psalm xxxiii. 10.

[3] Galat. v. 6.

might attain to the glory of the heavenly kingdom.[1]

[1] It is owing in great measure to this virtuous education given by Margaret to her sons that Scotland was governed for the space of 200 years by seven excellent kings, that is, by her three sons, Edgar, Alexander, David, by David's two grandsons, Malcolm IV. and William, and William's son and grandson, Alexander II. and III.; during which space the nation enjoyed greater happiness than perhaps it ever did before or after. (Cf. Mr Innes, "Sketches of Scottish History," p. 158; Mr Hill Burton, "History of Scotland," vol. ii. pp. 190-198; Mr Robertson, "Scotland under her Early Kings," vol. ii. pp. 171-180.)

Orderic ("Migne," vol. 188, p. 620) wrote panegyrics on the three brothers, and especially on David; but it is William of Malmesbury who is most emphatic on the unparalleled purity of life of all three. One child only, Edmund, is spoken of as falling away from the bright example of his parent. But Edmund repented sincerely, and became a monk at Montacute, a monastery founded by William the Conqueror in Somersetshire. (Cf. "Will. Malms. Gest. Reg. Angl.," v. § 400.)

The princesses, Matilda and Mary, were placed by their uncle Eadgar in the Abbey of Romsey, of which his surviving sister, Christina, was abbess. A few years later she followed her aunt Christina to Wilton Abbey, which was the place of nurture and education for many young princesses of the Anglo-Saxon royal families.

RUINS OF THE ROYAL PALACE, DUNFERMLINE.

CHAPTER II.

HER CARE FOR THE HONOUR OF THE REALM
AND THE DISCIPLINE OF THE CHURCH.

§ 12.

OR need we wonder that the queen governed herself and her household wisely when we know that she acted always under the wisest of masters, the guidance of the Holy Scriptures. I myself have had frequent opportunities of admiring in her how, even amidst the distractions of lawsuits, amidst the countless cares of state, she devoted herself with wonderful assiduity to the study of the word of God, respecting which she used to ask profound questions from the learned men who were sitting near her. But just as no one among them possessed a deeper intellect than herself, so none had the power of clearer expression. Thus it very often happened that these doctors went from her wiser men by much than when they came. She sought with a religious earnestness for those sacred volumes, and oftentimes her affectionate familiarity with me moved me to exert myself to obtain them for her use.[1] Not that in doing this she cared for her own salvation only; she desired that of others also.

§ 13. First of all in regard to King Malcolm: by the help of God she made him most attentive to the works of justice, mercy, almsgiving, and

[1] In the Middle Ages the Bible was comparatively seldom formed into one volume, and more commonly existed in its different parts. Even in the earliest periods we meet with notices of translations of numerous portions of the Inspired Writings into the various modern languages, and many copies of these different versions are still in preservation. We know of translations of the Bible into sixteen modern languages, made between the fourth and fifteenth centuries; and these must obviously have been written for the use of the laity, since the Scriptures were read by the monks and clergy in Latin, then the universal tongue of learned Christendom. Such, indeed, was often the openly avowed object. Thus Ælfric avers that he rendered the Scriptures into the vernacular "For the Edification of the Simple, who Know only that Language" (MSS. Camb. Wanley, 153). On this subject see Maitland's celebrated work "The Dark Ages," p. 187, *et seq.* (Cf. L. A. Buckingham's "The Bible in the Middle Ages," L. 1853, p. 45, *et seq.*)

other virtues. From her he learnt how to keep
the vigils of the night in constant prayer; she
instructed him by her exhortation and example
how to pray to God with groanings from the
heart and abundance of tears. I was astonished,
I confess, at this great miracle of God's mercy
when I perceived in the king such a steady
earnestness in his devotion, and I wondered how
it was that there could exist in the heart of a
man living in the world such an entire sorrow
for sin. There was in him a sort of dread of
offending one whose life was so venerable; for
he could not but perceive from her conduct
that Christ dwelt within her; nay, more, he
readily obeyed her wishes and prudent counsels
in all things. Whatever she refused, he refused
also; whatever pleased her, he also loved for the
love of her. Hence it was that, although he
could not read, he would turn over and examine
books which she used either for her devotions or
her study; and whenever he heard her express
especial liking for a particular book, he also
would look at it with special interest, kissing it,
and often taking it into his hands. Sometimes

he sent for a worker in precious metals, whom he commanded to ornament that volume with gold and gems, and when the work was finished, the king himself used to carry the book to the queen as a loving proof of his devotion.

§ 14. The queen on her side, herself a noble gem of royal race, much more ennobled the splendour of her husband's kingly magnificence, and contributed no little glory and grace to the entire nobility of the realm and their retainers. It was due to her that the merchants who came by land and sea from various countries brought along with them for sale different kinds of precious wares which until then were unknown in Scotland. And it was at her instigation that the natives of Scotland purchased from these traders clothing of various colours, with ornaments to wear; so that from this period, through her suggestion, new costumes of different fashions were adopted, the elegance of which made the wearers appear like a new race of beings.[1] She

---

[1] Hence, Lord Hailes conjectures that perhaps we owe to her the introduction of what we call Tartan. (Hailes, "Ann. Scot.," vol. i. p. 37.)

also arranged that persons of a higher position should be appointed for the king's service, a large number of whom were to accompany him in state whenever he either walked or rode abroad. This body was brought to such discipline that, wherever they came, none of them was suffered to take anything from anyone, nor did they dare in any way to oppress or injure country people or the poor. Further, she introduced so much state into the royal palace, that not only was it brightened by the many colours of the apparel worn in it, but the whole dwelling blazed with gold and silver; the vessels employed for serving the food and drink to the king and to the nobles of the realm were of gold and silver, or were, at least, gilt and plated.

§ 15. All this the queen did, not because the honours of the world delighted her, but because duty compelled her to discharge what the kingly dignity required. For even as she walked in state, robed in royal splendour, she, like another Esther, in her heart trod all these trappings under foot, and bade herself remember that beneath the gems and gold lay only dust and ashes.

D

In short, in her exalted dignity she was always especially watchful to preserve humility. It was easy for her to repress all vain glory arising from worldly splendour, since her soul never forgot how transitory is this frail life. She always bore in mind the text which describes our condition in this our unstable humanity: " Man, born of a woman, living for a short time, is filled with many miseries. Who cometh forth as a flower and is destroyed, and fleeth as a shadow, and never continueth in the same state."[1] She meditated without ceasing upon that passage of the Blessed Apostle James, where he asks: " What is our life? It is a vapour which appeareth for a little while, and afterwards shall vanish away."[2] And because, as the Scripture says, " Blessed is the man that is always fearful,"[3] this worthy queen made it easier for her to shun sin by placing ever before her soul's eye, tremblingly and fearfully, the terrible day of judgment. With this thought she frequently entreated me to rebuke her without any hesitation in private whenever I saw anything worthy of blame either

[1] Job xiv. 1, 2.   [2] St Jas. iv. 15.   [3] Prov. xxviii. 14.

in her words or her actions. As I did this less frequently and sharply than she wished, she urged the duty on me, and chid me for being drowsy (so to speak) and negligent in her regard; " for," as she said, " the just man shall correct me in mercy and shall reprove me; but let not the oil," that is, the flattery, " of the sinner fatten my head."[1] " Better are the wounds of a friend than the deceitful kisses of an enemy."[2] She could speak thus because she courted censure as helping to her progress in virtue, where another might have reckoned it a disgrace.

§ 16. Journeying thus onwards towards the heavenly country in thought and word and deed, this devout and god-worthy queen called on others to accompany her in the undefiled way, so that they with her might attain true happiness. When she saw wicked men she admonished them to be good, the good to become better, the better to strive to be best. The zeal of God's house (that is, of the Church) had so consumed her that with apostolic faith she laboured to root up all weeds which had lawlessly sprung up

[1] Ps. cxl. 5.   [2] Prov. xxvii. 6.

therein. Observing that many practices existed among the Scottish nation which were contrary to the rule of the right faith and the holy customs of the universal Church, she caused frequent councils to be held, in order that by some means or other she might, through the mercy of Christ, bring back into the way of truth those who had gone astray.

§ 17. Among these councils the most important is that in which for three days she, with a very few of her friends,[1] combated the defenders of a perverse custom with the sword of the Spirit, that is to say, with the word of God.[2] It seemed as if a second Helena were there present, for as that queen in former days by citing passages from the Scriptures overcame the Jews, so in our times did Queen Margaret overcome those who were in error. In this

---

[1] The names of those friends are not given by Turgot. But we know from other sources that Margaret had requested Lanfranc, Archbishop of Canterbury, to become her spiritual father. In conformity with this request, Lanfranc despatched to her three of his brethren, the senior being the English Goldwine, or Godwin, who were to lay the foundation of a renovated establishment. (Letter of Lanfranc to Queen Margaret, "Migne, Patres Latini," Sæc. xi. Col. 549.)

[2] Ephes. vi. 17.

discussion the king himself took part as an assessor and chief actor, being fully prepared both to say and do whatever she might direct in the matter at issue. And as he knew the English language quite as well as his own, he was in this council a very exact interpreter for either side.

§ 18. The queen introduced the subject under discussion by premising that all who serve one God in one faith along with the Catholic Church ought not to vary from that Church by new or far-fetched usages. She then laid it down, in the first place, that the fast of Lent was not kept as it ought to be by those who were in the habit of beginning it on the Monday of the first week in Lent; thus differing from the Holy Catholic Church, which begins it on the fourth day of the previous week at the commencement of Lent. The opponents objected thus: "The fast which we observe we keep according to the authority of the Gospel, which reports that Christ fasted for six weeks." She replied by saying: " Herein you differ widely from the Gospel, wherein we read that our Lord fasted for forty days, a thing which notoriously you do not do. For seeing that during the six weeks you deduct the six Sundays from the fast, it is clear that thirty-six days only remain on which to fast. Plainly, then, the fast which you keep is not that fast of forty days which is commanded by the Gospel, but consists of six and thirty days only. It comes then to this, you ought to do as we do. Like us, you should begin your fast four days before the first Sunday of Lent; that is, if you wish, according to our Lord's example, to observe an abstinence of forty days. If you refuse to do this, you will be the only persons who are acting in opposition to the authority of our Lord Himself and the tradition of the entire Holy Church." Convinced by this plain demonstration of the truth, these persons began henceforth the solemnities of the fast as Holy Church observes them everywhere.

§ 19. The queen now raised another point; she asked them to explain why it was that on the festival of Easter they neglected to receive the Sacrament of the Body and Blood of Christ according to the usage of the Holy and Apostolic Church? They answered her thus: " The Apostle when speaking of persons who eat and drink unworthily, says that they eat and drink judgment to themselves.[1] Now, since we admit that we are sinners, we fear to approach that mystery, lest we should eat and drink judgment to ourselves." "What!" said the queen to them; "Shall no one that is a sinner taste that holy mystery? If so, then it follows that no one at all should receive it, for no one is pure from sin; no, not even the infant, who has lived but one day upon the earth. And if no one ought to receive it, why did the Lord make this proclamation in the Gospel? 'Except you shall eat the flesh of the Son of Man and drink His Blood, you shall not have life in you.'[2] But if you would understand the passage which you have quoted from the Apostle according to the interpretation of the Fathers, then you must give it quite a different meaning. The Evangelist does not hold that all sinners are unworthy of the sacraments of salvation; for after saying 'He eateth and drinketh judgment to himself,' he adds, 'Not discerning the Body of the Lord;'[3]

---

[1] 1 Cor. xi. 29.   [2] St John vi. 54.

[3] 1 Cor xi. 29.

that is, not distinguishing it by faith from bodily food. It is the man who, without confession and penance, and carrying with him the defilements of his sins presumes to approach the sacred mysteries, such a one, I say it is, who eats and drinks judgment to himself. Whereas we who many days previously have made confession of our sins and have been cleansed from their stains by chastening penance, by trying fasts, by alms-giving and tears—approaching in the Catholic faith to the Lord's Table on the day of His Resurrection, receive the Body and Blood of Jesus Christ, the immaculate Lamb, not to judgment but to the remission of our sins, and as a health-giving preparation for eternal happiness." To these arguments they could not answer a word, and knowing now the meaning of the Church's practices, observed them ever after in the sacrament of salvation.

§ 20. Again, there were certain places in Scotland in which Masses were celebrated according to some sort of strange rite, contrary to the usage of the whole Church. Fired by the zeal of God, the Queen attempted to root out and abolish this custom, so that henceforth, in the whole of Scotland, there was not one single person who dared to continue the practice.[1]

It was another custom of theirs to neglect

[1] Turgot, unfortunately, does not say in what the strangeness of the rites consisted. On this subject, says the late Dr Forbes, we cannot do better than quote the words of that learned antiquary, the Right Reverend Bishop Kyle: "The contemporary biographer of St Margaret tells us that certain priests in Scotland followed, in celebrating Mass, a rite which to him and the Queen appeared barbarous ; which rite she laboured so effectually to abolish, that none in Scotland in his time adhered to it. I suspect that in this last point he was mistaken. For we learn that the Keledei (*Cele De*, one who has devoted himself to the service of God), long after St Margaret's days, were permitted to observe in their own churches or chapels a rite different from what was followed by the rest of the Scottish clergy. The rite of the Keledei was probably the same with that which St Margaret wished to bring into conformity with the general use of the Western Church ; but neither her biographer nor the chronicles of the Culdean observance give us the least hint wherein its peculiarity consisted. (Lib. Ecclesiæ B. Terrenani de Arbuthnot, p. liv.) There is no mention of Culdees in Scotland until the ninth century, as Chalmers testifies. They were secular canons who had been established since the ninth century. But although they were for the most part clerics, the name seems to have been given also to pious, unmarried laymen, inasmuch as they formed a community, and lived together. The later Bollandists have likewise come to the conclusion that they

the reverence due to the Lord's Day by devoting themselves to every kind of worldly business upon it just as they did upon other days. That this was contrary to the law, she proved to them as well by reason as by authority. "Let us venerate the Lord's Day," said she, "because of the resurrection of our Lord, which happened upon that day, and let us no longer do servile works upon it; bearing in mind that upon this day we were redeemed from the slavery of the devil. The blessed Pope Gregory affirms the same, saying : 'We must cease from earthly labour upon the Lord's Day and we must devote ourselves entirely to prayer, so that upon the day of our Lord's resurrection we may make expiation for such negligences as we may have committed during the six days.'"[1] The same Father, Gregory, after censuring with the greatest severity a certain piece of worldly busi-

were secular canons or brothers, and appeared, at soonest, in the year 800. (Bollandists, vol. viii., Oct., p. 86 : Disquisitio in Culdæos, cf. Dr Reeves, "The Culdees of the British Islands," Dublin, 1864.)

[1] "Ep. S. Gregorii Magni," lib. xiii., c. 1 opp. ii. p. 1214, ed. Bened.

ness which had been done on the Lord's Day, decreed that the persons who had advised it should be excommunicated for two months. The arguments of the queen were unanswerable; and from this time forward those prudent men paid such respect to her earnestness that no one dared on these days either to carry any burden himself or to compel another to do so.

§ 21. Next, she proved how utterly abominable, yea more to be shunned by the faithful than death itself, was the unlawful marriage of a man with his step-mother, as also that the surviving brother should take to wife the widow of his deceased brother; both of which customs had heretofore prevailed in the country. In this council she succeeded in condemning and expelling from her realm many other inveterate abuses which had gained a footing therein, contrary to the Rule of Faith and the institutions and observances of the Church. For everything that she proposed she supported so strongly by the testimony of the Sacred Scriptures and the teaching of the holy Fathers, that no one on the opposite side could say one word against them;

nay, rather, giving up their obstinacy and yield-
ing to reason, they willingly consented to adopt
all she recommended.[1]

[1] Even the smallest circumstances of every-day life were
sought out by St Margaret and put to spiritual profit. Having
observed that many neglected to give due thanks to God after
meals, she introduced the practice of drinking a health at rising
from table to those who had complied with that duty. Hence
this cup was called the *Grace Drink,* or St Margaret's Blessing.
A similar custom is related in some Anglo-Saxon chronicles.
On high festivals and other solemn occasions, to the abbot or
prior of the monastery there was brought a large bowl filled
with wine, of which he drank a little, and handed this
"poculum charitatis," or love-cup, to his monks, each of
whom took a short draught in like manner: after this cere-
mony, which was meant as a symbol of brotherly affection and
good will one towards another, was said grace, which finished
with a prayer for their benefactors alive and dead (Cod. Dip.
Anglo Sax. v. iv., p. 304). A relic of this Anglo-Saxon
custom may yet be seen in the grace-cup of the universities,
and the loving-cup passed round among the guests at the great
dinners given by the Lord Mayor of London.

Not many years ago, in Germany as well as Belgium, this
custom was still kept up, of sending round the loving-cup at
grace after dinner. Cf. Rock, "The Church of our Fathers,"
vol. ii. p. 335 *et seq.*)

CHAPTER III.

§ 22.

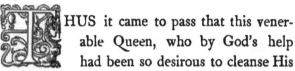

HUS it came to pass that this venerable Queen, who by God's help
had been so desirous to cleanse His
house from all filth and error, was found day by
day worthier of becoming His temple, as the Holy
Spirit shone ever brighter in her heart. And I
know of a truth that she was such, because I not
only saw the works which she did outwardly,
but besides this, I knew her conscience, for to me
she revealed it. It was her good pleasure to con-
verse with me on the most familiar terms, and to
open her secret thoughts to me ; not because there
was anything that was good in me, but because

she thought there was. When she spoke with me about the salvation of the soul and the sweetness of the life which is eternal, every word she uttered was so filled with grace that the Holy Spirit, Who truly dwelt within her breast, evidently spoke by her lips. So deep was her contrition that whilst she was talking, she seemed as if she could melt away in tears, so that my soul, pierced like her own, wept also. Of all living persons whom I know or have known she was the most devoted to prayer and fasting, to works of mercy and almsgiving.

§ 23. Let me speak first of all about her prayerfulness. In church no one was so silent and composed as she, no one so wrapt in prayer. Whilst she was in the house of God she would never speak of worldly matters, or do anything which savoured of the earth; she was there simply to pray, and in praying to pour forth her tears. Only her body was then here below, her spirit was near to God, for in the purity of her prayer she sought nothing but God and the things which are God's. As for her fasting, I will say this alone, that the strictness of her abstinence brought upon her a very severe infirmity.

§ 24. To these two excellent gifts of prayer and abstinence she joined the gift of mercy. For what could be more compassionate than her heart? Who could be more gentle than she towards the necessitous? Not only would she have given to the poor all that she possessed; but if she could have done so she would have given her very self away. She was poorer than any of her paupers; for they, even when they had nothing, wished to have something; while all her anxiety was to strip herself of what she had. When she went out of doors, either on foot or on horseback, crowds of poor people, orphans and widows flocked to her, as they would have done to a most loving mother, and none of them left her without being comforted. But when she had distributed all she had brought with her for the benefit of the needy, the rich who accompanied her, or her own attendants, used to hand to her their garments, or anything else they happened to have by them at the time, that she might give them to those who were in want; for she was anxious that none should go away in distress. Nor were her attendants at all offended nay rather each strove who should first offer her what he had, since he knew for certain that she would pay it back two-fold. Now and then she helped herself to something or other out of the King's private property, it mattered not what it was, to give to a poor person; and this pious plundering the King always took pleasantly and in good part. It was his custom to offer certain coins of gold upon Maundy Thursday and at High Mass, some of which coins the Queen often devoutly pillaged, and bestowed on the beggar who was petitioning her for help. Although the King was fully aware of the theft, he generally pretended to know nothing of it, and felt much amused by it. Now and then he caught the Queen in the very act, with the money in her hand, and laughingly threatened that he would have her arrested, tried, and found guilty. Nor was it towards the poor of her own nation only that she exhibited the abundance of her cheerful and open-hearted charity, but those persons who came from almost every other nation, drawn by the report of her liberality, were the partakers of her bounty. Of a truth then this text may be applied to her, "He hath dispersed abroad, he hath given to the poor, therefore his justice remaineth for ever."[1]

§ 25. But who can tell the number of English of all ranks, carried captive from their own land by violence of war and reduced to slavery,[2] whom she restored to liberty by paying their ransom? Spies were employed by her to go secretly through all the provinces of Scotland and ascertain what captives were oppressed with the most cruel bondage, and treated with the greatest inhumanity. When she had privately ascertained where these prisoners were detained, and by whom ill-treated, commiserating them from the bottom of her heart, she took care to send them speedy help, paid their ransom and set them at liberty forthwith.

[1] Ps. cxi. 9.

[2] So great was the desolation of England after the conquest, that many became slaves to any one who would feed them. Remigius, Bishop of Lincoln, and St Wulfstan, Bishop of Worcester, preached against the wicked custom by which men sold their country-folk, sometimes their kinsfolk, to a life of shame or of bondage in foreign lands. (Giraldus, "Vita Rem.," c. 3, 4, 5.) The slave trade was severely condemned by the council of London in 1103. ("Mansi Collectio Concil.," xx. p. 1152.)

E

§ 26. At the period of which we are speaking, there were in many places throughout the realm of Scotland persons shut up in different cells, and leading lives of great strictness; in the flesh, but not according to the flesh; for being upon earth, they led the life of angels. These the Queen busied herself in often visiting and conversing with, for in them she loved and venerated Christ, and would recommend herself to their prayers. As she could not induce them to accept any earthly gift from her, she urgently entreated them to be so good as to bid her perform some alms-deed or work of mercy, and this devout woman did forthwith fulfil whatever was their pleasure, either by helping the poor out of their poverty or by relieving the distressed in their troubles, whatever these might be.[1]

[1] Some of these Anchorites were her own Saxon country-men, driven by the Norman conqueror into exile. Although seclusion and continual prayer have been practised by Christians in all ages since the commencement of the Church, yet the eremitical life has assumed its external form principally as the result of persecutions. Like the days of which the Apostle wrote to the Hebrews, "they wandered about in sheep-skins, in goat-skins, being in want, distressed, afflicted, of whom the world was not worthy : wandering in deserts, in mountains, and

§ 27. Since the church of St Andrews was much frequented by the devout, who flocked to it from all quarters, she erected dwellings on either shore of the sea which divides Lothian from Scotland, so that the poor people and the pilgrims might shelter there and rest themselves after the fatigues of their journey. She had arranged they should there find all that they needed for the refreshment of the body. Servants were appointed, whose especial duty it was to see that

in dens, and in caves of the earth " (Heb. xi. 37). Many who thus began this life under compulsion found so great a sweetness in uninterrupted intercourse with God, and in the perfect subjection of the body to the soul, that they clung to it when they might have returned to an easier mode of life. " It is probable that among those Anchorites who commended themselves so much to her favour were the *Cele De* of Lochleven, for we find Malcolm and Margaret, king and queen of Scotia, giving devoutly the town of Ballechristin to God the Omnipotent and the *Keledei* of Louchleven, with the same liberties as before. ("Chart. Prior, S.A.," p. 115.) Bishop Fothad too (here called Modach, son of Malmy Kel, a man of most pious memory, bishop of St Andrews, with whose life and doctrine the whole region of the Scots was happily enlightened), gives to God and St Servanus and the hermit *Keledei* on the island of Lochleven, living there in the school of all virtues, devoutly and honourably, with the same liberties, the church of Auchterderran." ("Chart. Prior, S.A.," p. 117; W. F. Skene, "Celtic Scotland," vol. ii. p. 351.)

everything which might be required for these way-
farers should be always in readiness, and who
were directed to attend upon them with all dili-
gence. Moreover, she provided ships for the
transport of these pilgrims both coming and going,
nor was it lawful to demand any fee for the
passage from those who were crossing.

§ 28. Having spoken of the daily manner of
life of this venerable queen, as well as of her
daily works of mercy, it is fitting that I should
now attempt to say a few words as to the way in
which she habitually spent the forty days before
Christmas, and the entire season of Lent. After
taking rest for a short period at the beginning of the night, she went into the church,
and there, alone, she completed first of all the
Matins of the Holy Trinity, then the Matins of
the Holy Cross, and lastly the Matins of Our
Lady. Having ended these, she began the offices
of the Dead, and after these the Psalter; nor did
she cease until she had reached its conclusion.
When the Priests were saying the Matins and
Lauds at the fitting hour, she in the meantime
either finished the Psalter she had begun, or if she

had completed it, began saying it a second time. When the office of Matins and Lauds was finished, returning to her chamber, along with the king himself, she washed the feet of six poor persons; and used to give them something wherewithal to relieve their poverty. It was the chamberlain's special duty to bring these poor people in every night before the queen's arrival, so that she might find them ready when she came to wait upon them. Having done this, she went to take some rest in sleep.

§ 29. When it was morning she rose from bed and devoted a considerable time to prayer and the reading of the Psalms, and while thus engaged, she performed the following work of mercy. She ordered that nine little orphans utterly destitute should be brought in to her at the first hour of the day, and that some soft food such as children at that tender age like, should daily be prepared for them. When the little ones were carried to her she did not think it beneath her to take them upon her knee, and to get their pap ready for them, and this she put into their mouths with the spoon which she herself used.

The queen, who was honoured by all the people, did this act of charity for the sake of Christ, and as one of Christ's servants. To this most loving mother might be applied with great propriety that saying of the blessed Job, "From my infancy mercy grew with me, and it came forth with me from my mother's womb." [1]

§ 30. While this was going on, it was the custom to bring three hundred poor people into the royal hall, and when they were seated round it in order, the king and queen entered; whereupon the doors were shut by the servants, for with the exception of the chaplains, certain religious and a few attendants, no one was permitted to be present at the giving of these alms. [2] The

---

[1] Job xxxi. 18.

[2] That this access to her might be easier, she is said to have frequently sat in an open field, where every one who pleased might have an opportunity of speaking to her with greater freedom; and there is still shown, on the road to Queensferry, rather more than a mile from Dunfermline, a stone in the form of a seat, which, according to a constant tradition, she sometimes made use of for that purpose. It is marked in the maps of the roads published not long since, as being near the fourteenth mile from Edinburgh, with the name of *St Margaret's Stone* affixed to it. ("The Life of St Margaret," by the Right Rev. T. Geddes, Aberdeen, 1794, p. 34.)

king on the one side and the queen on the other waited upon Christ in the person of His poor, and served them with food and drink which had been prepared for this special purpose. When the meal was finished, the queen's wont was to go into the church, and there with long prayers, with tears and sighs to offer herself as a sacrifice to God. Upon holy days, in addition to the hours of the Holy Trinity, the Holy Cross, and Holy Mary, recited within the space of a day and a night, she used to repeat the Psalter twice or thrice; and before the celebration of the Public Mass she caused five or six Masses to be sung privately in her presence.

§ 31. These concluded, it was time for the queen's repast. But before this was served she herself humbly waited upon twenty-four poor people whom she fed; for without reckoning the alms-deeds which I have already mentioned, throughout the course of the year she supported twenty-four poor as long as she lived. It was her will that wherever she lived they also should be living in the neighbourhood; wherever she went they were to accompany her. Not until after she had devoutly waited upon Christ in these His poor was it her habit to refresh her own feeble body. In this meal she hardly allowed herself the necessaries of life, since the Apostle teaches us that we ought not to make provision for the flesh in its concupiscences.[1] She ate no more than sufficed for the preservation of her life, and not to gratify her palate. Her meal— frugal and scanty—rather excited hunger than allayed it. She seemed to taste her food, not to take it. From this let it be understood, I pray you, how great was her abstinence when she fasted, remembering what it was when she feasted. Her whole life was one of exceeding temper- ance, but during the fasts (that is during the forty days before Easter and Christmas), the abstinence she was accustomed to afflict herself with was incredible. By reason of this excessive severity she suffered to the end of her life from an acute pain in the stomach ; yet the weakness of her body did not impair her strength in good works. During this period she was assiduous in reading the sacred volumes, she was instant in prayer, her

[1] Rom. xiii. 14.

alms were unceasing, and she exercised herself wholly and watchfully in all the things of God. And knowing, as she did, that it is written: "Whom the Lord loveth He chastiseth, and He scourgeth every son whom He receiveth,"[1] she willingly accepted with patience and thanksgiving the pains of the flesh, regarding them as the stripes of a most loving Father.

§ 33. Devoted as she was to such works as these, and burdened by the like constant infirmities, God's power was made perfect in her weakness.[2] Thus passing onwards from strength to strength, each day made her better. And now forsaking all things earthly with her whole soul, she longed for the things of heaven, yea, thirsted after them, exclaiming with the Psalmist in the language both of her heart and lips, "My soul hath thirsted after God, the living fountain; when shall I come and appear before the face of God?"[3] I leave it to others to admire the tokens of miracles which they see elsewhere, I admire much more the works of mercy which I perceived in Margaret; for signs are common to

---

[1] Prov. iii. 11, 12.   [2] 2 Cor. xii. 9.   [3] Ps. xli. 3.

the good and the bad, whereas works of piety and true charity belong to the good only. The former sometimes are the proof of holiness, the latter are that which constitutes it. Let us then, I repeat, admire in Margaret the actions which made her a saint, rather than the miracles which, had we any record of them, would have proved that she was one. In her character let us observe with admiration the works of the ancient Saints rather than their miracles—her justice, her piety, her mercy, and her love. Yet it will not be out of place if I here narrate one incident which may go to prove what the holiness of her life was.

§ 33. She had a book of the Gospels beautifully adorned with gold and precious stones, and ornamented with the figures of the four Evangelists, painted and gilt. All the capital letters throughout the volume were radiant with gold. She had always felt a particular attachment for this book; more so than for any of the others which she usually read. It happened that as the person who carried it was once crossing a ford, he let the book, which had been carelessly folded in a wrapper, fall into the middle of stream. Unconscious of what had occurred the man quietly continued his journey; but when he wished to produce the book, suddenly it dawned upon him that he had lost it. Long was it sought, but nowhere could it be found. At last it was discovered lying open at the bottom of the river. Its leaves had been kept in constant motion by the action of the water, and the little coverings of silk which protected the letters of gold from becoming injured by contact with the leaves, were swept away by the force of the current. Who could have imagined that the book was worth anything after such an accident as this? Who could have believed that so much as a single letter would have been visible. Yet of a truth, it was taken up from the middle of the river so perfect, so uninjured, so free from damage that it looked as if it had not been touched by the water. The whiteness of the leaves and the form of the letters throughout the volume continued exactly as they had been before it had fallen into the stream, except that on the margin of the leaves, towards the edge, the least possible mark

of damp might be detected. The book was conveyed to the queen, and the miracle was reported
to her at the same time; and she, having thanked
Christ, valued it much more highly than she had
done before. Whatever others may think, I
for my part believe that this wonder was worked
by our Lord out of His love for this venerable
queen.

THE FRATER HALL, DUNFERMLINE ABBEY.

CHAPTER IV.

THE QUEEN'S PREPARATION FOR HER DEPARTURE,
HER SICKNESS AND HAPPY DEATH.

§ 34.

WHILST Almighty God was preparing everlasting rewards for her works of devotion, the queen was preparing herself with more than her usual assiduity for entering another life. Her own words made this more obvious shortly afterwards. It would seem that her departure from this world, as well as certain other events which were impending, had been known by her long beforehand. Therefore, summoning me to come to her privately, she began to recount to me in order the history of her life, and as she proceeded with it she shed floods of tears. In short, so deep was her compunction, and out of this compunction sprang such abundant tears, that—sa it seemed to me—

there was nothing whatever which at that time she might not have obtained from Christ. When she wept, I wept likewise; and thus we wept and at times were silent altogether, since by reason of our sobs we could not give utterance to words. For the flame of that compunction which consumed her heart reached my soul also, borne in thither by the spiritual fervour of her words. And when I heard the language of the Holy Ghost speaking by her tongue, and could thoroughly read the tenderness of her conscience by what she said, I judged myself unworthy of the grace of so exalted a familiarity.[1]

§ 35. When she had ended what she had to say about matters which were pressing, she then addressed herself to me, saying: "I now bid you farewell. I shall not continue much longer in this world, but you will live after me for a consider-

---

[1] Instead of the above paragraph, Capgrave's abridgment of this biography, printed also by Surius, has as follows: "Habebat confessarium Turgotum, secundum Priorem Dunelmiæ. Illi ergo ad se accersito, vitam suam replicare cœpit, et ad singula verba lachrymarum flumina profundere; tantaque erat sub ejus sermonibus compunctio, tantus lachrymarum imber, ut nihil proculdubio esse videretur, quod tunc a Christo impetrare non posset." This is copied by Pinkerton, p. 381.

able time. There are two things which I beg of you. One is, that as long as you survive you will remember me in your prayers; the other is, that you will take some care about my sons and daughters. Lavish your affection upon them; teach them before all things to love and fear God; never cease instructing them. When you see any one of them exalted to the height of an earthly dignity, then, as at once his father and his master in the truest sense, go to him, warn him lest through means of a passing honour he become puffed up with pride, or offend God by avarice, or through prosperity in this world neglect the blessedness of the life which is eternal. These are the things, said she, which I ask you—as in the sight of God, who now is present along with us both—to promise me that you will carefully perform. At these words I once more burst into tears, and promised her that I would carefully perform her wishes; for I did not dare to oppose one whom I heard thus unhesitatingly predict what was to come to pass. And the truth of her prediction is verified by present facts; since I survive her death, and I see her offspring elevated to dignity and honour. Thus, having ended the conference, and being about to return home, I bade the queen my last farewell; for after that day I never saw her face in the flesh.

§ 36. Shortly afterwards she was attacked by an infirmity of unusual severity, and was purified by the fire of a tedious sickness before the day on which God called her to Himself. I will describe her death as I heard it narrated by a priest of hers, whom she loved more intimately than the others on account of his simplicity, his innocence, and his purity. After the queen's death he made an oblation in perpetual service for her soul, and having put on the monk's habit offered himself up as a sacrifice for her at the tomb of the uncorrupt body of the most holy Father Cuthbert. He was continually beside the queen during the last days of her life, and with his prayers recommended her soul to Christ when it was leaving the body. He gave me more than once a connected narrative of her decease as he saw it, for I frequently asked him to do so; and in doing this he was moved to tears.

§ 37. "For a little more than half a year," said he, " she was never able to ride on horse-back, and seldom to rise from her bed. On the fourth day preceding her death, while the king was absent on an expedition, and at so great a distance that it was impossible for any messenger, however swift, to bring her tidings of what was happening to him, she became sadder than usual. Then she said to me, for I was seated near her, ' Perhaps on this very day such a heavy calamity may befall the realm of Scotland as has not been for many ages past.' When I heard these words I paid no great attention to them, but a few days afterwards a messenger arrived who told us that the king was slain on the very day on which the queen had spoken the words narrated. As if foreseeing the future, she had been most urgent with him not to go with the army, but it came to pass—how I know not—that he failed to follow her advice.[1]

[1] We have no very clear account of the immediate cause which led to the open breach between William and Malcolm. But it is plain from the Peterborough Chronicle that William was in the wrong, and refused to do something for Malcolm which he had promised to do. Malcolm entered the earldom

§ 38. "On the approach of the fourth day after the king's death, her weakness having somewhat

of Northumberland, and ravaged it after his usual fashion as far as some point which, there is no reason to doubt, was in the near neighbourhood of Alnwick. We may fairly accept the tradition which carries him to the spot known as Malcolm's Cross, where a commemorative rood was erected, and where the ruins of a Romanesque chapel may still be seen. The spot is on high ground overlooking the river Alne, while on the opposite side of the stream a lower height is crowned by the town of Alnwick, and by such remains of its famous castle as modern innovation has spared. By ambush or some other stratagem Earl Robert of Mowbray led his forces against the Scottish king unawares, under circumstances which are not detailed, but which have led even English writers to speak of the attack as treacherous. Malcolm was killed; and with him died his son and expected heir, Edward. The actual slayer of Malcolm was his gossip Morel, Earl Robert's nephew and steward, guardian of the rock and fortress of Bambrough. (E. Freeman, "The Reign of William Rufus," vol. ii. p. 15.) Simeon of Durham says that he was cut off near the river Alne, and that "part of his army fell by the sword, and part escaping the sword were carried away by the inundation of the river, then more than usually swollen after the winter rains. Two of the natives placed the body of the king in a cart, as none of his men were left to commit it to the ground, and buried it at Tynemouth. Thus terminated his long reign of thirty-five years." (Cf. Sim. Dun. de Gest. Reg. ad an. 1093.) By some of the Scotch chroniclers Malcolm is said to have been slain at Inneraldan, by others at Alnwick.

The character of Malcolm was variously regarded by the

abated, the queen went into her oratory to hear
Mass; and there she took care to provide herself
beforehand for her departure, which was now so
near, with the holy Viaticum of the Body and
Blood of our Lord. After partaking of this
health-giving food she returned to her bed, her
former pains having assailed her with redoubled
severity. The disease gained ground, and death

English and by his own subjects. The English historians,
who had mainly to record his frequent invasions of Northumberland, regarded him as a man of barbarous disposition,
delighting, at the instigation of his avarice, to ravage and de-
vastate the northern districts of England; while they attributed
any better traits in his character to the humanising influence of
his consort Queen Margaret. By his Celtic subjects he was
known as Malcolm Ceanmor, or great head, and was esteemed,
according to the testimony of St Berchan, as

> " A king, the best who possessed Alban ;
> He was a king of kings fortunate.
> He was the vigilant crusher of enemies.
> No woman bore or will bring forth in the East
> A king whose rule will be greater over Alban ;
> And there shall not be born for ever
> One who had more fortune and greatness."

On his death he left the kingdom in possession, for the first
time, of the same southern frontier which it ever after
retained. (F. Skene, "Celtic Scotland," vol. i. pp. 431,
432.)

was imminent. . . . Her face was already covered
with a deadly pallor, when she directed that I,
and the other ministers of the sacred Altar along
with me, should stand near her and commend
her soul to Christ by our psalms.   Moreover, she
asked that a cross, called the Black Cross,[1] which
she always held in the greatest veneration, should
be brought to her.   There was some delay in
opening the chest in which it was kept, during
which the queen, sighing deeply, exclaimed,
'O unhappy that we are!   O guilty that we
are!   Shall we not be permitted once more to
look upon the Holy Cross!'   When at last it
was got out of the chest and brought to her, she
received it with reverence, and did her best to
embrace it and kiss it, and several times she
signed herself with it.   Although every part of
her body was now growing cold, still as long as
the warmth of life throbbed at her heart she continued steadfast in prayer.   She repeated the
whole of the Fiftieth Psalm, and placing the cross

---

[1] "Crucem Scotiæ nigram," Brit. Mus. MS. Tiberius,
E. i. 186a.

before her eyes, she held it there with both her hands.[1]

§ 39. "It was at this point that her son,[2] who now, after his father, holds in this realm the reins of government, having returned from the army, entered the queen's bedroom. Conceive his distress at such a moment! Imagine to yourself how his heart was racked! He stood there in a

---

[1] The Black Cross was enclosed in a black case, whence it was called *the Black Cross*. The cross itself was of gold, and set with large diamonds. "It is about an ell long," says Aelred, "manufactured in pure gold, of most wonderful workmanship, and may be shut and opened like a chest. Inside is seen a portion of our Lord's Cross (as has often been proved by convincing miracles), having a figure of our Saviour sculptured out of massive ivory, and marvellously adorned with gold. Queen Margaret had brought this with her to Scotland, and handed it down as an heirloom to her sons; and the youngest of them, David, when he became king, built a magnificent church for it near the city, called Holy-Rood." (Bollandists, vol. xxi. p. 335.)

When Edward the First invaded Scotland, he seized on this cross as one of the English crown jewels, and carried it into England. Robert Bruce so vehemently demanded its restoration that Queen Isabella yielded it up on the pacification during her regency in 1327; but its surrender exasperated the English more than the most flagrant of her misdeeds.

[2] "Filius suus Edgarus." (MS. Tiberius, E. i., 186.)

strait; everything was against him, and whither
to turn himself he knew not. He had come to
announce to his mother that his father and brother
were both slain, and he found that mother, most
dearly beloved by him, at the point of death.
He knew not whom first to lament. Yet the
loss of his dearest mother, when he saw her
lying nearly dead before his eyes, stung him to
the heart with the keenest pang. Besides all
this, the condition of the realm occasioned him
the deepest anxiety, for he was fully aware that
the death of his father would be followed by an
insurrection. Sadness and trouble beset him on
every side.[1]

§ 40. "The queen, who seemed to the by-
standers to be rapt in an agony, suddenly rallied
and spoke to her son. She asked him about his
father and his brother. He was unwilling to tell
the truth, and fearing that if she heard of their
death she herself would immedia.ely die, he re-

___

[1] A party among the Scots hated the rule of Malcolm, as
being a favourer of Sassenaghs and foreigners; and a party
was already in arms preparing to besiege the Castle of Edinburgh.

plied that they were well. But with a deep sigh she exclaimed, 'I know it, my boy, I know it. By this holy cross, by the bond of our blood, I adjure you to tell me the truth.' Thus pressed, he told her exactly all that had happened. What could she do, think you? To murmur against God was with such a one impossible. At the same moment she had lost her husband and her son, and disease was bringing her to a cruel death, yet in all these things she sinned not with her lips, nor spoke foolishly against God. Raising her eyes and her hands towards heaven, she glorified God, saying, 'All praise be to Thee, Almighty God, who hast been pleased that I should endure such deep sorrow at my departing, and I trust that by means of this suffering it is Thy pleasure that I should be cleansed from some of the stains of my sins.'

§ 41. "Feeling now that death was close at hand, she at once began the prayer which is usually uttered by the priest before he receives the Body and Blood of our Lord, saying, 'Lord Jesus Christ, who according to the will of the Father, through the co-operation of the Holy Ghost, hast

by Thy death given life to the world, deliver me.'
As she was saying the words, 'Deliver me,' her
soul was freed from the chains of the body, and
departed to Christ, the author of true liberty; to
Christ whom she had always loved, and by whom
she was made a partaker of the happiness of the
saints, as she had followed the example of their
virtues. Her departure was so calm, so tran-
quil, that we may conclude her soul passed at
once to the land of eternal rest and peace. It
was remarkable that her face, which, when she
was dying had exhibited the usual pallor of death,
became afterwards suffused with fair and warm
hues, so that it seemed as if she were not dead but
sleeping.[1] Her corpse was shrouded as became a
queen, and was borne by us to the Church of the

[1] The place of her death is not mentioned by Turgot in the
Life. Fordun (v. 21) states that Margaret died in Edinburgh " in castro puellarum ; " and on the 16th of November
in the year 1093, according to the Chronicle of Mailros.
See also the Surtees " Simeon," p. 262. Wynton relates the
occurrence as follows :—

> " As thys dede all thys ware doune
> Come wything til Saynt Margret soune
> The Revelatyoune that west maist,
> That scho had of the Haly Gast.

Holy Trinity,[1] which she had built. There, as she herself had directed, we committed it to the grave, opposite the altar and the venerable sign of the Holy Cross which she had erected. And thus her body at length rests in that place in which, when alive, she used to humble herself with vigils, prayers, and tears."

END OF TURGOT'S LIFE.

The public opinion of Margaret's sanctity had already prevailed all over Britain for the space of more than one hundred and fifty years, when it received the sanction of Pope Innocent IV. in the

> Than wyth devot and gud intent
> Scho tuk the Haly Sacrament
> Of Goddis Body blyst wërray
> Wyth the last unctyoune ; and that dai
> Of al charges scho yhald hyr gwyte
> And til the Creatoure hyr Spyryte
> In-til the Castelle of Edynburgh," etc.

(Wynton's " Orygynale Cronikil," vol. ii. pp. 271, 272.)
[1] Dunfermline Abbey.

year 1250. On that occasion, and on the 19th of June of that year, the body of the saint was taken up from the grave, where it had hitherto lain, and was placed in a silver shrine, adorned with precious stones, which was deposited under the high altar of the church.[1]

" According to Papebroch's appendix to the life of the saint and queen, her head was brought to the Castle of Edinburgh at the desire of Queen Mary, who was staying there at the time, and on her flight into England in 1567 it was removed to the house of the Laird of Dury, where it was preserved for many years by a Benedictine monk, until in the year 1597 it was by him given up to the missionary Jesuits. One of these, John Robie, conveyed it to Antwerp. There John Malder, Bishop of Antwerp, after due examination, issued his letters, on 15th September 1620, authenticating the head as that of St Margaret, and granting leave for its being exposed to public veneration. After seven years the relic was translated to the Scots College at Douay, where, by permission of Herman, Bishop of Arras, and his

[1] Brev. Abd., 19 Jun.

successor, Paul Boudot, it was again exposed as a genuine relic to public veneration. Pope Innocent X., by a brief dated March 4th, 1645, granted a plenary indulgence to those who should visit the church of the college on the festival of St Margaret, and this grant was confirmed by his successors at various times afterwards. It is believed that this relic disappeared amid the commotions of the French Revolution.[1]

" With regard to the other remains of Queen Margaret and her husband, if we may believe the accounts given by Papebroch, which he seems to have partly, if not wholly, derived from a statement by George Con, in his treatise, 'De Duplici Statu Religionis apud Scotos,' they were, after much labour, acquired by Philip II., King of Spain, and by him placed in the Church of St Lawrence at the Escurial, with the inscriptions, 'St Malcolm, King; St Margaret, Queen,' on the urns containing them. Bishop Gillis, in the

---

[1] In 1785 it was still at Douay, where the historian Carruthers saw it at the Scotch College. It continued in extraordinary preservation, with a quantity of fine hair, fair in colour, still upon it.

hope of having the relics of St Margaret again restored to a Scottish shrine, invoked the aid of Pius the Ninth in an application to the Spanish Government for their restoration, but they could not be found, or at all events identified."[1]

[1] "Transactions of the Antiquarian Society of Scotland," ii. 89. Cf. Bishop Challoner, "Britannia Sancta"; Alban Butler, "Lives of the Saints," vol. vi., June 10, Edinburgh edition, 1709, p. 154.

ST MARGARET'S CAVE.

CPSIA information can be obtained
at www.ICGtesting.com
Printed in the USA
BVHW030817270819
556806BV00017B/13/P